Versus

MW01717097

Versus

Stacia M. Fleegal

BlazeVOX [books]

Buffalo, New York

Versus by Stacia M. Fleegal

Copyright © 2011

Published by BlazeVOX [books]

All rights reserved. No part of this book may be reproduced without the publisher's written permission, except for brief quotations in reviews.

Printed in the United States of America

Book design by Geoffrey Gatza
Cover photo by Tom Dieffenbach

First Edition
ISBN: 978-1-60964-043-9
Library of Congress Control Number 2010934395

BlazeVOX [books]
303 Bedford Ave
Buffalo, NY 14216

Editor@blazevox.org

N
W E
S

publisher of weird little books

BlazeVOX [books]

blazevox.org

2 4 6 8 0 9 7 5 3 1

BlazeVOX

Acknowledgments

Thanks to the editors of the following journals who published poems from this manuscript:

Babel Fruit, “Spending My Inheritance from Whitman”
Blue Collar Review, “Pilgrimage”
Fourth River, “Visitor’s Pass to Bedlam”
The Heartland Review, “Storm Element” and “Synesthete”
Inkwell, “Candlelight Dinner in India”
The Kerf, “Not Your Typical Praise Poem”
Mobius: The Journal of Social Change, “Saving the World?”
New Verse News, “Your Story of ~~Two Centuries~~ Ten Minutes Ago”
Pemmican, “Outside of This Blue Line, You Aren’t Homeless,” “The Mutes Begin to Breathe Fire,” and “The Day I Am Fingerprinted at the Sex Shop”
Prick of the Spindle, “The Heresy of Silence”
Protest Poems, “The War of All against All” and “Instruction Manual for a Revolutionist”
Skidrow Penthouse, “Bavarianna”
Slurve, “Bear Grylls Survives the Republican National Convention circa 2004,” “Fuck the Bourgeoisie,” and “To the Reluctant Feminist"

Some of these poems appear in the chapbook *The Lines Are Not My Friends*, which was awarded second place in the 2009 Cervená Barva Press chapbook competition and published in March 2010; so many thanks to Gloria Mindock and William J. Kelle at CBP. Thanks to the editors of *The Kerf* for nominating “Not Your Typical Praise Poem” for a Pushcart Prize in 2009.

To my first readers of this book: Teneice Durrant Delgado, John Steele, Tom Dieffenbach, and Dan Nowak, thank you for your honesty, insight, and enthusiasm. Dan, you inspire me to name names, loudly and without fear. You have my love and admiration always.

Table of Contents

For everyone who remembers.

I've never read a political poem that's accomplished anything.
-Howard Nemerov

Last night you wrote on the wall: Revolution is poetry.
Today you needn't write; the wall has tumbled down.
-Adrienne Rich

Versus

Vs.

What sits in the V of Vs. is what I want,
a sun in a valley. What divides, rides
the bridge. What curls up in S,
that cave, that yin yang.
What crawls so re-
luctantly to a
perio-
d
.

Pretty Decoy

Racing for Pinks

Always we want the greener lawns of others—
the neighbors wear out their blinds by spying,

their finger oils weakening the vinyl
as if it were a museum's ancient text

on Atlantis, Rome, or England. Who's next?
Lipstick-shiny SUVs and hi-def,

Blu-ray, digital, "life-like"—life's like
a movie set, or children painting

refrigerator boxes set as scenery for
a skit everyone pretends is brilliant, modern,

not mechanical. Pay no attention
to that man behind the cardboard curtain.

Forget this all goes on our credit cards
and we own nothing. Faux Mrs. Jones

waters her plastic begonias, scolds
the teenage boys drag-racing daddy's

mid-life-crisis-mobile while daughters
begin stripteasing, cardigans discarded

on porches. Always a girl at the end waving
a part of herself in the greasy air to show

the precise spot of both winning and losing.

Spending My Inheritance from Whitman

Because there was nothing controversial about you, Walt,
and since the world's most lucrative career path is poetry,

I am on my way to the bank to cash my inheritance
check. They want ID. I take off my clothes.

They want a bit of blood. I give them ink
and they can't tell the difference. I can't believe

the line isn't longer—where are your other children?
I was hoping to catch glimpses of some here. Later,

I plan to hand out plays by Oscar Wilde outside
churches. I'm going to try to like Pound more.

I'm going to buy a new Civic hybrid and
a million fountain pens, then go to visit

Dickinson's home in Amherst. I'm going
to hire a pool boy. I might even get a pool.

I'll register to take a class on flag-making.
And then, the way some drive Kerouac's Route 6,

I'm going to walk the path you took
in December 1862 to get to your soldier brother,

whom you thought dead, but found instead
with a beautiful face-paint wound. I'm not

going to talk to anyone along the way, just walk a war
line, pocket picked, toeing elegies into the mud.

The Great american Male Identity Crisis

I.

Five of us in a friend's living room:
a single woman,
a hetero couple,
a gay couple,
and then the two guys who
show up with the pot, frat brothers,
silver chains and ball caps,
good buds, eyeing
her chest and my ass.

Seven now.
The gay men put away their wallets
and leave the room.
My partner stays, his hand on
the back of my neck.

II.

We are moving and the new neighbors
tell us they were mugged last week.
It is a city hit hard by recession.
It is a city that hits hard.
The woman was hit hard in the throat.

In my new bed, I can't not see her: she is
face-down, she sees cigarette butts and litter
and light trails and is squirming to stay
in her pants, in her body, alone in her body,
unskewered. My guts ache for the rape
that didn't even happen.

Just the fact of this thought,
and the way I check the knuckles
of every man I pass.

III.

A coworker tells me her son
hates

to cry,
fights
it, punches

doors.

IV.

At the grocery store, when
my partner and I split the bill,
the male cashier doesn’t know
whether or not to hold

the door open for me
as I struggle with
a heavy bag. We
both consider
asking for ID.

Fuck the Bourgeoisie

We ARE the bourgeoisie,
she counters, giggling. Is it
my new jacket? Her
advanced degree?

I don't know what they are
teaching her in comp/rhet, but my wisdom
tooth is rotting at my jawbone,
rotting like an empire,

and my father's teeth are all gone,
the pain and bills vying to outlast
each other. She thinks she knows Marx
but has never heard of McGrath,

or Joe Strummer. I'm not bothered
that her iPod playlist (or price tag)
is different than mine, or that her
education is already paid for, or that

her teeth are beautiful and spell
university insurance. What pisses me off
to no end is not her Coach bag dreams,
but how she steers the topic to gay rights

and crucifies anyone who is out but not
a bulldog activist. That she does this
on break from writing her dissertation on
how we are "post-patriarchy," while

I am Jason Bourne spying every exit
that frames a drunk guy eyeing
her party dress thighs. If I am not
a worker, who is? What makes me

want to burn down that cherry-picked library
and light a joint with Ezra Pound embers,
or at least donate this new faux leather to Goodwill,
is how she included me.

Fingerprinting the Innocent

When I make my lines headlines, I don't
want you to flip to the sports pages—or worse,

believe you're already on them when you read
about rape and war. What I can't ignore

is america's classifieds. Wanted:
non-co-opted freedom. A night street

I'm not afraid of, and short skirts only I
can see, because my legs are beautiful

unsplayed and they deserve the sun, the moon,
the air, and if I'm on my knees before

whatever I choose to worship, the dirt.
What can't you ignore? I know it's hard when

even black and white lies: a woman spends
24 years locked in a soundproofed basement

having her father's seven children, but
MSNBC won't use the word *rape*.

It happened in Austria; will you say
other countries' problems are not ours?

Diplomacy is no fair-weather friend,
and it doesn't always rain on war protests.

How large is your umbrella? It's raining
hate everywhere, and I huddle under

a night club's awning in Lawrence, Kansas,
long after my cigarette sizzles out.

A woman crosses the street alone. She could
be my sister. *Sister*, I want to call her

back, buy her a paper, protect her from
the newsprint blackening our whorls, our world.

The Day I Am Fingerprinted at the Sex Shop

is just like any other day—I am longing
for touch and it is being used against me.

The government is keeping track of those who
are having good sex. If that list were longer,

maybe I wouldn't be this store's only Sunday
patron with the perfect purple four-speed egg

and tapping my bank card on the counter's edge
while, still in the box, the cashier tests it,

swipes my card, prints a receipt, asks me to sign and
smudge my body onto paper. I want to

say to the surveillance camera: this
is what I do every day. You have my

name, is that not enough? Should I also
say female orgasms are a myth? (My name

begins to break from itself, separating
like oil from cream.) Or that I'd rather have

the phallus than the roundness my palm
controls? (My print unwhorls. Ink and I

shape-shift.) See? I can lie past fingerprints.
You'll never know it was me. I'm just a receipt.

Synesthete

I. Submit (a color-coded past)

S is red
T is green
A is pink
C is yellow
I is…
A is pink again

I am four and
words and colors
teach each other to me.

I won't learn
the name for this
until much later. Right now,

I am concentrating.
Hug the lines with my color.
Don't upset the teacher.

I try not to, but she
asks me to make the I blue,
to not repeat the pink. *No,*

I is not M or W.
I am not blue.
(I am being difficult.)

I am mostly pink and green,
and won't learn these are heart chakra
colors until much later.

II. Rebel (much later)

From this point on, I will not tolerate
intolerance. I will not look away
from the gray middle ground, will rub my hands
in the dirt of it so I don't forget.

Rules and their exceptions teach each other
to me. The lines are not my friends. I will not hug them, but redraw them
with a tough love pat on the ass and a well-wish.
I'll keep them, though, little quartzes. They're mine.

I need them to tell you about futures
we envision from color-coded pasts—
mine, yours, the Salem witch's, the first moon's.
A white tongue dipped in black would be my tomb.

To hell with death. To hell with quiet life.
That was not the volta, by the way.

To hell with every word not being a turn.

A Word Person Playing a Numbers Game

Countdowns and weather love math:
100,000 dead in Burma's cyclones,
8,000 lost to China's earthquakes.
Here, where we care less and less,
Obama gets 2 more superdelegates.

There is a 60 percent chance of apathy
in the Midwest, where our own weather
and 4 dollar gallons of gas ruin
vacation plans. 3,000 lost to Katrina,

but what strength of gale stirs empathy in
americans? Our leaders scream *stimulate!* as if
trying to direct an orgy. We can't even

afford eggs. 5 more months of Bush, 4 more
primaries, 3 candidates, 2 parties, 1 poverty line.

Gas just hit 4 and a quarter.

The War of All against All

after Hobbes and a line by Glenn Sheldon

The day before we sign the social contract,
we are all at the anarchists' picnic
trying to figure out why no one's
shown up. I bring egg salad sandwiches.

We are all at the anarchists' picnic
to learn Latin—*bellum omnium contra omnes.*
I show up with egg salad sandwiches
but they are just smooth, fist-sized stones.

My Latin omits *bellum, contra. Omnes*
I understand. We can't all agree on
whether they're smooth, fist-sized stones
or bats or bludgers used for beating rebels.

I understand we can't all agree, but
let's at least eat. No (yes)? A food fight, then?
Bats for bludgeoning and beaten rebels
abound in states of nature AND of war.

Let's at least eat our words like food, and fight
tomorrow, when we sign the social contract.
Is it a state of nature or of war?
Who tries to figure it out, and why? No one.

Golden Boy

after *Baron's Hill* (2004), a series of photographs of the ornamental cast brass and wood ingots of the homes of the Sorocan wealthy elite, at the 21C in Louisville, KY

Two feet tall, I just know you would be
fair-haired, blue-eyed, even if you weren't
a privileged Moldovan child—a regal house,

balcony of perfect bricks, all for show,
for partying, not living?—and nothing impish
about the look on your face as you do it.

But for now, let's say how you are preserved:
shameless gilded boy on your stone perch,
eye-level with skyscrapers, even gods,

and gripping your stump of a phallus
like how the gardener your parents underpay
would hold a hose, only harder, and you're

enjoying it more—not *that* much, but
I have to wonder at your eyes, the cold blue I
again know they'd be, but still hard, still iron,

wide as a full-grown man's when he's possessed
by his possessions. So I stand in this museum,
in america, drinking a soy chai latte in my Gap jeans,

thinking how you'd grow up here thinking
you could be a cowboy, or even president,
going over all our heads to piss on the whole world.

Bear Grylls Survives the Republican National Convention circa 2004

It's the opposite of a Tom Cruise movie:
a non-american invited to show us how it's done.
To evaluate his effectiveness in lost cause
military endeavors, you should know Bear Grylls
isn't into quick, utilitarian exits.

Welcome, then, to america!
If you want to learn how to survive
a rogue presidency, lesson number one is:
don't eat the food. Apple pie, fried chicken,
spinach, tomatoes, or peanut butter, you'll only
contract dysentery and consumerism.
Also, it's colder than you'd imagine. Bear suggests
stealing fire and brimstone from Pat Robertson,
but if all else fails, pilfer fuel from
Condi's namesake Chevron tanker.
It's parked out back with all the SUVs.

Now, he'll want to show you how to get out
of a really sticky situation, and the best way
is if he just bellows, *Let the gays get married!*
Then you can actually watch him backpedal
out of death-stares with useful, well-timed quips
like *More disposable income for the churches!*

When you see Rush Limbaugh, whatever you do,
don't look him in the eye. Back away slowly.
No matter how much you want to tell him
how minor he is, your safety is more important.

Practice the hearty belly laugh of the privileged
so it doesn't seem as contrived as a war speech.

In dire times, you may be forced to bite off the head of
an Iraqi child to preserve democracy.

Day two, and the fire's really going now.
Watch him get the public's attention with smoke-
screens to win the trust of the suits and—
he's always wanted to try this—see if
spewing random trivia works
to instill panic in republics better than in
Brazilian rainforests, where there are almost
as many deadly snakes.

Almost. Even a man named Bear
knows about playing dead, about
not being seen OR heard (Big Brother,
or covert wire-tapping), and after three days
of trying to tame errant elephants,
Bear Grylls faces america, exhausted, to say,
I've really gained an appreciation for
those of you who endure these elements.
Then Thirsty will leave Power-Thirsty, depart for Britain
where he'll murder nothing larger than a cup of tea.

Prime Time

Topomax, Flonase, Fosomax, Activase,
Enzyte, Ativan, Folvite, Percodan,
Yasmin, Xanax, Codeine, Chantrix,
Depo Provera, Humera, Strattera.

Avodart, Darvocet, Adenocard, Percocet,
Diflocan, Plavix, Zyban, Celebrex,
RotaTeq, Lipozene, Zyrtec, Benzedrine,
Imitrex, Miralax, Nasonex, Zovirax,

Urex, Ambien, Valtrex, Claritin,
Gardisil, Adderall, Elavil, Nembutal,
Glucotrol, Maxair, Nicotrol, Advair,
Nexium, Nizoral, Lithium, Demerol,

Ultram, Nasocort, Zicam, Symbicort,
Glumetza, Novacaine, Lunesta, Lidocaine,
Rozerem, Viagra, Somatrem, Allegra,
Spiriva, Abreva, Sustiva, Boniva...

Outside of This Blue Line, You Aren't Homeless,

after learning about "panhandling zones" painted on sidewalks in Orlando, FL

For there aren't enough prisons / to lock up all the poor. -Czeslaw Milosz

just breaking the law. You'll need to learn to
beg with borders; boxes drawn on sidewalks
are a child's game. But this is not a game.
This is your life on pharmaceutical drugs—

so deadly you can't believe it's legal.
Politicians say you could've had more
foresight, should've foretold the foreclosures.
Funny the clairvoyance they expect before

they arrest you for reading palms on Main Street.
Seventeen floors up, on Wall Street, they're toasting
their luck. How does a person stay in a
box if the lines are drawn with white-out?

So they make them flag-stripe blue so they stand out
and the workers work and work   but can't get out.

Pilgrimage

The american jobs are braving the Pacific and Atlantic
in rickety little boats.

They are guilty of associating with the working
poor, and so must seek

asylum in India. The jobs are fearful—they carry
six figures and the boats are

already collapsing under their weight, their
pilgrimage to "a better place."

They are alone. At least they will not suffer the fate
of their lower-wage friends:

gobbled up by ravenous young families with
student loan debt and no closet

space in foreclosed homes to stuff a splintered
american dream—can't recycle it

or they'll be jailed and the jobs absorbed into
these white collar seas.

The boats, too, quiver between swells. They have only
one duty, one leaking job.

Drawing the Line with Invisible Ink

Inversions

We are so used to seeing what we are
making take the shape of what it will be
the moment we turn making hands on it—
gradually, it begins to look more
and more like itself, how it will be.
It is the most logical way, some say.

But the die-for-art glassblower knows best:
that a hard knot of glass gone molten,
petted, cradled, rolled tirelessly round,
rebels against symmetry, but can be
cajoled back, warmed, and whirled, and then re-warmed,
with specks of color spinning out freeform.

That we only stop becoming when we cool,
and just breathing changes all we thought we knew.

Farce Poetica

I use the word *filament* at least twice.
Nothing says how futile my poetry
is like *filament*: threadbare. Formulaic
as cross-stitches. Scoff all you want—there IS
a sapling underneath an ancient oak
in my backyard, and it DOES inspire all,
makes a celebrity guest appearance
in each poem you'll dissect for meaning. Don't.
Not without filaments, quicksilver, or
reading my blurbs (there's one from Christian Wiman!).
Not smoke, not mirrors—look over there for those.
And substance: breasts, revolutions, punched timecards.
Here, there's only a workable sapling.
Listen. The rotting oak is telling it how to die.

Are These Poems Alive?

I heard a line buzz
when I died—
and Dickinson
lives on.

But will my lines
survive
as more than—
mere imitation?

This Poem Begs the Revolution for a Job

Leo Marks was a Special Ops chief cryptographer during World War II who revolutionized the use of ciphers after learning about them as a child from the Edgar Allan Poe story "The Gold Bug."

Use me. I am worthy. Hide in me
        all the things you'd say if

being a poet was still dangerous. I am
        dangerous. I am

a direct descendant of Leo Marks,
        and I can bear the code.

I can be elusive and I look great in black.
        I've been dying for a moon-

lighting gig as an acrostic because
        I've spent too much time horizontal

and all the blood has rushed from my head.
        Make me think. I can make

people think I'm nothing. Just a poem.
        Only you will know

that I'm the absolute and perfect truth.
        Use me. Don't use invisible ink.

Instruction Manual for a Revolutionist

Don't be afraid of paper cuts or bullet holes,
or people who don't consider these the same.

You carry the cosmos in your eyes and ears.
It is they who should fear you, pilgrim.

This is about waiting: watch the dollar fall,
the sun rise, all things certain. In the meantime,

learn a trade. Religion's now helpful only
to those who can't do magic, who huff

and puff and gasp, then call it sin. Eat
with gusto. Sit in coffee shops and people-watch,

hear inanities' ease, slow-drip anger—stay
with me, here, for I've seen what you'll say

kills, but I've seen it save; rage can rage on
against age and playing safe, silence, and chafed

lips bitten straight. Seek not to build bombs
in these folds, but to change into your kamikaze

cape and be one, or a dragon. Study. Make
so much love. Memorize the constellations, then

chart new ones with pegs on which to hang
this list, so when you've finished, you can

burn these pages. They'll never think
it was you, pretty decoy: flammable flesh.

In Defense of Anger

america is the quietest land of all the lands. Our billboards
say yes for us, no to the opposite of what's on them.

The others wall-hug, whisper about you, think they're being
noncontroversial because they hide their mouths.

You're wearing red. You wear red every day.
The garment has no seams, seems neither to begin

nor end. You're the Hester Prynn
of american insouciance. Shame

says you should look like her, but shops
in the same non-corporate stores as you. Bliss thinks

you're invisible. Your parents, Awake and Depressed,
whine *Why can't you be more like your sister Suicidal?*

And where are your old friends?—Idealist, that sweet dreamer,
and Control Freak, who was finally managing his OCD?

They lost your number when they switched to Verizon.
You turned around and painted it in the sky, and not in blue,

or with that cryptic ink that's only seen by lightning light,
but red (what else?). It may be your very blood. Won't

Desperation finally emerge from the crowd like a chameleon
dropping the background, stand with you back to back as if

you were scrappy dogs cornered but making ready for a fight?
You're willing to tear your clothes. The garment has no seams.

In Defense of Antagonizing People

In football, the tip of the nose tackle's nose
is the starting point of a metaphor
about peace. Yes, the good game ass-slap
always involves taking sides. See,

it starts at a drawn line, then whittles up
from there: two faces both determined not
to let the other cross; their likeminded
behind them; an arena of colors;

the cameras as windows for the ticketless
opinions; larger causes—competition,
entertainment, and finally, making
people smile. Peace in screaming. Pick a team.

Know this: crowd noise is always a factor.
Wear your choice loud and proud, you might end up
on the big screen. Lines are meant to be crossed—
it's why we have to keep redrawing them.

(It's why even a pacifist feminist
needs Sundays to feel connected to west
coasters and weekend warriors—war terms
on my lips make sense when chased with lager

and confined to boxes with off buttons.)
Would you live in a world with only
participation trophies? No. Someone
must win. Start the wave if you care who it is.

The Call

Thank you for calling Heaven. For security purposes,
this call will be monitored.

For English, please stay on the line.

Main menu.
For a prophet, press 1.
For Jesus, press 2.
For God with a capital G, press 3.

3.

Please hold while we find the next available
preacher to field your call. In the meantime,
if you know your preacher's extension,
you may enter it now.

If you're calling to report a sin, press the pound key.
If you're calling to request the fulfillment of a prayer,
please stay on the line, your continued patience is appreciated.
If you're doing God's Work and are checking in,
please press star.

Star.

We're sorry, all circuits seem to be busy, but
whatever you do, you must stay on the line.

Answering the Call

I have stood in a field of lavender
and studied a doe's corpse like ancient text

that won't translate. I have eaten every
kind of apple. Why can't you tell me what

part of speech *why* is? And why withhold phone
books? Somewhere, someone must be hoarding them.

I suppose I can understand why we need gods,
but I can't understand the grammar of it—

drop the plural, capitalize the G,
never the feminine ending. By the third

ring of The Call, I wonder if most people
are so weary of question marks that even

a dangling participle will suffice:
calling all sinners, god doesn't speak to mortals.

I suppose I can understand this. I suppose
I would pick up the phone just to ask who it is.

I Do

reject all institutions with built-in
discrimination: the flesh-colored
bandage industry, and marriage, that
bastion of homophobia. When hatred

of the feminine in either women or men
turns publicly ugly, let's cover it with matrimonial
gauze, let's let it fester and think we've saved it.
Let's read *US Weekly* to learn ourselves—Britney's

marital jaunt was quirky, but my gay friend's lover
lies dying in a hospital and no one will give
a "life partner" (the nurse finger-quotes it)
information, so he waits, thumbs

through the waiting room tabloids, wishes
he had long blonde hair extensions and a drug problem.

I Don't

Marriage is only a sin when those who can't have it
want it. Make me understand that. And the priest
who wouldn't marry my sister and her
boyfriend because they already cohabit.

And why celebrities embody hetero-
normalcy. And how MTV can promote
teen weddings like iPods. And why people
who beat their children have tax breaks and god

on their side. And how the stat for divorce
doubles the one for rape and neither's a crime.
And how quickie Vegas weddings and quickie
Mexican divorces are more moral than

just quickies. Anyone have a guess? Bet you
a blood diamond I don't, I don't, I don't.

Gerontophobia

Someday, says this old white guy,
you'll want
to write

about anything but
yourself,
politics,
childhood,
bodies,
sex.

Old white guy,
get your
hand off
my thigh.

Bad Riddle

Predictable as a falling empire, futile as a new year's
resolution. What hypocrisy
e
v
e
n-
tually gets us all, youth-hater, drained of fight?
I'm doing what you once did, eve-
n if you've forgotten: breaking the
goddamn clocks and hoping it fells the clockmakers.

Die then, if you won't help, won't admit what's
even more
artificial
than living, more
human than breath.

Elegy for Hillary's Campaign, June 4, 2008

Coffins are unfortunately too small
for the entire media, which is pushing
everyone to bury you instead. I won't.
I cried for women today—Goliaths
always win when Davids wear pantsuits, and you
were always the underdog, the bitch.
They call you "former frontrunner" now
and penis-pump the open VP slot.
I know why you never say the word *feminist*,
and I forgive you, but I won't shut up.
MSNBC says what you want can only be
given by him. What is a win if it's granted
instead of earned? What should we hope for?—
to be given the right to earn, or to learn
to love second, and the cool dirt on our faces?

Your Story of ~~Two Centuries~~ Ten Minutes Ago

We are two hundred and thirty-two years old,
I want to say, but only the wake of your story
would hear because the girl is long gone who
said the thing that, as you relay it now,
tires me with ache—I literally want
to lie down and wake up draped in rainbows
and see the girl and hear her say, *Colors,*
can you forgive me? But instead, she said,

I can't vote for him because he is black.
She actually used the word *can't.* I can't
fathom hate while sitting next to you, love,
or even alone after you have to leave.
Earlier, you said he's like Kennedy.
Neither comment conjures the word *free.*

An Unknown Poet's Grandiose Call to Action

If all the living world is your canvas and

you can see where there is red earth and
you can hear where there is white noise and
you can taste orange and yellow fruits and
you can smell purple in a hard-earned spring and
you can feel night-time or rainbows and

you can hug your children and
you can joke about incompetent leaders and
you can relate to suffering and
you can feel remorse and
you can stockpile food in your basement and
you can worship your television and
you can answer your phone when it rings and
you can buy things with promises and
you can never run out of promises and
you can promise that and

you can hear about Darfur and Burma and Lebanon and
Detroit and St. Louis and Mexico and
Kosovo and genocide and holy wars and
rape-as-a-weapon and hate crimes and
drowned polar bears and extinct butterflies and
dead uninsured children and jobs outsourced and
everyone everywhere casting stones and

you can sleep at night and

you can brandish the tool you were given at birth on this soil and
you can appreciate art when being cultured is "in" and
you can testify that pictures on menus deepen hunger and
you can see the merit of having the whole picture

how then does your brush still hang lamely at your side?

The Poet's One Reader Fires off an Email

Do you feel better now, poet?
        Sure you do, you think you're better
        than me. Wish I had time to paint pictures.
        I work, see. You don't want children? I have three.

Do you feel better now, poet?
        Sure you do, bringing me here, so far from
        the suburbs, to dole out blame and shame.
        You're the first stone, casting yourself.

Do you feel better now, poet?
        Sure you do, if poems are penance.
        Aren't poems supposed to rhyme? Yours didn't.
        Isn't penance supposed to bring humility?

Do you feel better now, poet?
        Well, you shouldn't. For all your finger-
        paintings, you didn't save a single
        polar bear, rape victim, or world.

Back to Glass

To see a face, one must have a face.
To see another, one must be, and an-
other must be, too. Which is real? Both,
or neither. But not one or The Other.

One thing cannot have balance. Two are required.
The underground. *Viva la resistance.*
Anti-anything. *History repeats,*
and *For each dark night, a bright day lies ahead.*

There must be love to be love unrequited.
And what if every mirror's double-sided?
How are your eyes when the breath-fog's not so hot?
No need to do what that old advice says:

your enemies, those you've hated, slandered, fought,
are close whether you keep them there or not.

Flammable Flesh

Versus

I. Co-mplicit

I hate you
for showing me hate
on a sunny day with no chance
of rain, father of my often fatherless
love, when so many chances for love exist.

I hate you
for saying that black
man has no motivation outside of
taking drugs and making babies. For saying it
on Xanax, around a swill of Bud, from a porch swing.

I hate you
for not knowing your son,
the man he is beside the other men,
beside me in bed, beside the Jamaican family
next door, the father who brings his daughter peaches.

I hate you
for seeing nothing
outside your white town bubble,
for hyperbolic talk and drunkenness,
for my feeble, swollen, tender, bitten tongue.

I hate you
for the nasty way you
say *two guys, one truck* about
your neighbors, your jackass eyebrows,
and knowing we've just buried a dear gay friend.

I hate you
for infecting me with new
smells, dilated pupils. For making me
feel what you feel, for all our brazen evil,
both of us prancing around with our ugly showing.

II. Co-ntentions

That my grandma had the kindest hands
and her favorite slang was *cotton-pickin.*

That there's even talk about immigrants
and it's led by immigrant amnesiacs.

That I gave up meat seven years ago
and still miss bacon.

That a vice president has an inequality vice
and a gay daughter.

That the world is perched on a hot plate
and it's snowing more every winter.

That the language of tug-of-war for both is back
and forth.

That even bibles have both a recto
and a verso.

That an abortion clinic bomb kills a nurse
and a still-pregnant woman.

That all wars kill the guilty
and the innocent. And the innocent. And
the innocent. And the innocent.

That all the tree wants is up, up, up
and the air would starve the roots.

That I get into bed on the left side
and get out on the right.

III. Co-

She was on one side, I on the other,
the bed was the tangible thing between us.
She was blonde, pretty neck and knees.

He was the band and I was the crowd,
drum skin, his skin, my skin against the wall.
His hands were calloused, eyes black tourmaline.

Will you say, *pick one?* Impermanence
is the biggest taboo, after all. *Stand still,*
the label-makers' union strike is over!

I'm not bisexual and I'm not confused,
but if we could love women, we could love
anyone. V is pink in my mind's palette.

I try to say this to the camera. Response:
go back to the girl on girl. I try
to say it to america. Response:

you're straight, honey. Can you appreciate
the ease of her neck in my hands, or how
perfect, like an emerald, it all was?

Or that I wanted only that one night
with him, and was content to leave, loving
only hip bone bruises, beard-burned breasts?

For a warring nation, we sure hate
the V-word, how it sits between two ~~legs~~ rules
as if judged, an unmade bed the neighbors see.

These are not what poems ought to be.
The marketing's a bitch, they say, but this
is not negative space, this V.

Choose, they insist, as if they made that word
what it is. Man or woman. No loitering
in between.

Can't I just love with a capital V?

Saving the World?

Sure, I'll take a stab at it.
How about

butterflies? How about caring
that the Homerus swallowtail,

the largest of its genus in
the western hemisphere, is

nearly extinct?
Now, dilate

that feeling, like a camera
lens panning

a field of swallowtails. Make
that field mean something

bigger. Orange, maybe
fire flying. Pretend

you can't catch it
with nets. Let it burn.

Calling All Conscientious

arsonists. Bring your wisdom
to the government! The rules

on controlled burns are clear: it must
begin naturally. Couldn't we fake it?—

like an orgasm or suntan? Couldn't we just
march right in and steal it where they horde it?

Didn't someone do that once? Let's entrust
ourselves with tool belts in the aftermath

and welcome the torches' splinters. I imagine
they'll feel like tiny wooden stakes. But pluckable.

Staking a Claim

Helpmeets and hubris, the song on everyone's
pious tongues is the same as a summer
blockbuster's soundtrack: unwed non-virgins
die horrible deaths, screen seven, pew four.

Please, judge this book by its man-made cover.
Remember those dirty-kneed mornings you
bowed your head trying to see hell, but could
not un-know your own goodness, how you drew

you and your mom holding hands in permanent
marker on her pizzeria napkin,
that you fed your kitten every day,
that you held your pee through movies, church,

and meals. Even now, hard bread and bitter wine
depress you. (Not quite as much as when churches
insure their priests against molestation
charges while denying Magdalenes white

collars, but still, you like a hearty rye
and grassy Chardonnay.) And when the men
use altars, incense, candles, ancient texts,
ritual objects, parables, words like

sabbath, *sacrifice*, and *spirit* inside
buildings, you know that they'd condemn you for
doing the same thing in the woods. You might
glimpse the carpenters out there, building stakes.

The Heresy of Silence

The demands of Truth are severe... Unless incidentally, [Poetry] has no concern whatever with Truth or Duty... The true artist will always contrive to tone them down. Edgar Allan Poe, from *The Heresy of the Didactic*

Poe would've burned me at the stake.
He would've locked me in an elegy—
that pendulum between life and death—
for suggesting truth is relative
and as much itself as lies. Disguises
in poems? Hard-rhyming love is
anything but *cool, calm, unimpassioned.*
I was already a teacher at six
the moment his poems bit my hands; still,
I've only ever sat in classrooms.
Some alchemy makes pens didactic here,
between flexors and abductors. I may
stutter: Poe—poets
die, bindings crack out loud,
but at least flame enunciates.

The Grandmother Paradox

It doesn't take a quantum physicist
to understand that going back in time
and so much as stepping on a spider
could make the world to which the traveler

returns unrecognizable. We've all
seen *Back to the Future*; pop culture loves
this concept as much as beautiful girls
with slashed throats. So why is it so hard

to believe that the first women-lover
whose face was ground into the dirt she loved
by an invader's wheel and male war gods
would still exist, not just her bloodied daughters,

had the scout of the first south-moving tribe
been near-sighted, sitting on a spooked horse,
or looking right instead of left and not seeing
the sage smoke's mystic wisp amidst yew trees?

Magdala

An ancient bit of linen—cream, or red?
Truth is relative as women's shrouds.
Magdala means *tower of strength*
in Hebrew, but some hear only *tower.*

Mary, Mary, on the contrary, could
you have been a priestess, bower blessed?
Gnosticism's mystery insured
with tithes, you remain, like a gift rose, pressed

between the pages of an ancient book.
Could others believe books have lies, are
too perfectly box-shaped but won't hold
a single element? Or am I too late?—

and history has folded back once more,
and you're the archetypal whore.

Candlelight Dinner in India

Wet doe eyes and
        a pretty
tremble, she tries
        to cover
more of the floor
        with her skirt,
to befriend the dirt
        so she'll have
someplace to go once
        the sweet
kerosene embrace
        is over
and her husband snuffs
        the candle
out on her forehead
        where a kiss
goodnight should go.

Bavarianna

Your name was Anna Pappenheimer,
and I dreamed your fate from an american
living room the night before I bought
the obscure book cradling your story

like my recliner cradled me, a cup of tea,
a happenstance meeting between us.
Will I ever sleep well again? I dreamed
a room full of you, actually—naked,

hanging, breastless, tongues cut out, all wearing
tattered Victoria's Secret. I touch
the ties on my robe, the down lap blanket,
my eyelids. None of these cover you.

Bavarian ducal spies dressed you in lies
while stripping you before the thousands who
flocked from the countryside to see you rise
by the strappado, improvise your confession

for a quick respite from the pain. Your lips
only seemed to bleed from speaking falsely;
really, it was your amputated breasts, pressed
to your mouth, forced into your sons' mouths

to mock anything you'd ever meant to anyone.
I bite my lip and wish I tasted blood.
I cry for you, put loved women's faces
where yours is blurry in my head. So I

dreamed you, woke up, mourned you, plotted how to be
a storm crow cawing *Anna Pappenheimer.*
Then I bought a new book, got burned by the tea
kettle—how humane, steam instead of flame.

To the Reluctant Feminist

after Shelley's "To Wordsworth"

Woman of Fantasy, you don't want to know
that things return which never did depart:
the strength of women, the goddess's first glow
arrive like sweet dreams as if, with you, they start.
These common joys we feel. Pain theirs and mine,
which you deny and we alone deplore.
You are as a blind bird, whose wings are fine,
but who chooses to stumble rather than to soar.
We have like to a rock-built refuge stood
before a battling, bumbling apathy:
in silent poverty, we have withstood
those songs devoid of truth and liberty.
Enjoying rights at which you used to scoff,
we cannot help but be beyond pissed off.

It's Been Done

In writing groups, the word is *familiar.*
It is the kind synonym of *cliché.*

They don't mean *red as a rose.*
They mean rape. Rogue

governments. They mean
close your eyes. I crunch numbers:

eight women. Statistically, two raped.
Five men. I won't attempt that math.

You eight, is any of this *familiar*
to you? Are you angry?

You don't want to make people angry.
And why the fuck not?

You don't want built-in expiration dates.
My poems are not a carton of milk.

You eight, do you feel dated?
Courted, then violated?

How about this. I'll stop writing
rape when rape stops. You say

it's been done. You talk of endings.
I say you never finished the book

before writing the review, and
the book is always tomorrow.

So don't blame me, or these women.
Blame today for being yesterday.

The Mutes Begin to Breathe Fire

I.

Once we were warm in our beds. We were
covered with an epic quilt—maybe it was
made of words, maybe actual squares
of ourselves, portioned then collected

like so many berries from one tree.
It's like that parachute game we played as
kids: everyone with a fistful, and the fabric
heaved upwards, and the ring we danced,

and the effort was light because there were
so many of us. Over our heads, a sun
we'd all made...until one or two betrayed us,
darted out from under, pulled it down

and trapped us under our own foolishness,
yelling *Poisonous! The mushroom's poisonous!*

II.

I see a movie about a dead girl.
I see a movie about men, and there are dead girls.
I see a billboard with a bed girl.
I see a bed with a girl in it.
I see a girl with a bed in it, I mean, her.
I see a girl with a baby in her.
I see a mother eat a little girl.
I see a girl who won't eat.
I see a man rape a girl.
I see a hung jury.
I see a girl who hanged herself.
I see a girl who loves another girl.
I see a man get off on that.
I see a man pretend to get off on that.
I see the first man beat the second man.
I see a dead man.
I see a movie that won't be made.
I see a book that won't be read.
I see they're handing out ropes with the Constitution now.
I see a crystal ball turn smoky as a sky.

III.

The sound of feminism in 2008
    is a woman's scream during an illegal
    abortion in the same back alley where she was
    raped a few months before, choked
    with her handbag strap, unwrapped condoms strewn
    about the concrete like confetti.

The sound of feminism in 2008
    is a right-wing rally cry for family
    values, you know, like the celebrities have,
    every *OK!* Magazine cover blossoming
    like a uterus with pre-packaged
    Hi My Name is Woman labels.

The sound of feminism in 2008
    is a hammer brought down on
    the heads of women protesting
    media coverage of the Clinton campaign
    by the carpenters of Palin, who must
    be rescued after a mere five days of footage.

The sound of feminism in 2008
    is this chivalry, this old white straight male hand
    reaching down to pull up one token woman
    to sell to the rest of us as progress
    while our children die, our jobs set sail,
    our homes and books, our very flesh, it all burns.

IV.

Here is a book that won't burn: millions
of grassroots blogs, all with the same flag:
do they really think we're that fucking stupid?

Even if McCain could use the internet...
Even if Fox would broadcast these numbers...
Even if we all called out at once...

We are just discovering our eyes, but when
will ears be prerequisites,
when will voices be untaxable?

Visitor's Pass to Bedlam

for H

You lied and told me I could bring you cigarettes.
Maybe you didn't lie, I don't know how this works.
Did you or didn't you know yourself?

Anyway, I brought them. White coats made me
check them at the door. They went to fetch you,
but you were already peeking out, seeking noise.

Don't say anything about the cigs, you hissed, eyes
pricked like ears. You showed me your notebooks,
claimed 6,025 poems since December.

You wanted me to tell you about my sex
life, and when I joked about needing cigs
for that, too, you licked your lips, changed

the subject, told me—*reminded* me, your word—
that our mother, Madonna, had a birthday coming.
Forgive me for watching the cumulonimbus clouds,

worrying that I hadn't closed my moon roof,
instead of looking at your collection of magazine
cut-outs of people you think look like Jesus.

My mumbled apology was to the southern summer wind
because you became oblivious as rain. What dilated
your pupils if you hoarded pills like pennies?

We talked only of what you don't fear: *that bitch
from across the hall, with her night terrors,* who
threatened to punch you in your face. Then,

global warming. Clear, urgent: *I know you've been so worried,
I can sense it.* My psychic sister. And when
did I become the paranoid schizophrenic? *Mother*

Earth is just pissed off. First thunder crack. *No man can
destroy Her.* When you sighed like someone whose work
was done and leaned way back to give the space above us

your face, did you expect to feel drops? We
rested a long moment, breathed unpolluted air,
counted on our fingers for the lightning.

Even the Moon

Even the moon has a choice, changes
clothes—different robes for east and west.

Why should she apologize? Or the earth,
for having favorite colors?

The swell of a dirt-brown belly
doesn't always deserve someone's sweet smile.

A billion plastic whatever-wrappers choke even
the most calcified quartz, taproots, bones—time capsules

that never needed our input. One more of us stamping
her. One more of us landfilling and pillaging.

There is a woman in Arkansas or Tennessee
who just had her seventeenth baby.

She is all but gone, but the diapers could soak up
a man-made lake. And never decay.

I said no to children one blood moon day
then went swimming in a lake I didn't destroy

with chlorine or polyacrylates or lofty
narrow ideas of femaleness. Every toddler

has felled at least five trees—even without
my immortal blood, there are so many of us

and still, still we haven't found a way
to keep from shitting all over the planet.

You there. Will you call it judgment
when you stand before your maker

and tell her you're sorry about the methane
and oil and countless human synthetic toxins

and she drowns you anyway? No, you won't.
Even then, you won't understand that she's killing

her babies to save herself, and it's not pretty
or fun, but survival, and she has every right to do it.

Not Your Typical Praise Poem

Hail, the sky ice visits the earth
        to make puddles of itself
hail, the most emotionally cold
        of all the elements
hail wants to be rock, wants to be dirt
        but is just
hail, muddy quartz singing on
        a tin roof along a back road
hail knocks the summer leaves off their high
        horses, insists we don't forget winter, death
hail in Nebraska in August, Kansas in July
hail the megacryometeors, global climate change's
        gift to us in the form of giant
hail through my windshield into
        the loose change dish
hail is the cool currency of gods who want
        to buy the confusion of mortals who won't
hail them, regale them with epic
        weather poems about
hail, only sailing home from wars, wars, wars
        to be
hailed as heroes for conquering whatever
        can't conquer them, like
hail, sleet, snow, rain, ice, wind, fire, earth, storm,
        all of nature, mothering and strong—

hail the untameable, and how much
hail could the curtailed Antarctic shelf produce
hail for millennia, smashing down, suicide
hail is hell on the top of the head, so
hail the hail!

Storm Element

Storms combine the elemental forces of earth, air, fire, and water. Their transformative and healing powers are the strongest of all the elements separately.

I. Earth

Fix her. Just as she's fixed you with herbs, grains,
refuge, show her reverence. Stop this

matricide, lest she refuse your buriers entry.
The third planet could be a brilliant storm

if not for greed and capitalized gods.
Cradle her and try to tell her no.

Fight her and learn the source of *in thin air.*

II. Air

Accept what you can't see, but only if
it raises hairs on the back of your neck.

Breathe. Let others breathe. It's all the same
sweet saving, sans holy wars in desert wind

that tries to cover them with hourglass sand,
stirring it up so it doesn't singe our feet—

the wind cools because the sun burns.

III. Fire

Stop burning people and spreading hate with
threats of hell. There will never be enough

crosses. Candle flames need our altars, but
supernovas are immortal. (Love as if)

You aren't; rage like a fire-fighter
who believes steam's the end, not the start,

that white heat lets us better see cool blue.

IV. Water

Libation's almost liberation—bend
the word like a waterfall to this near-end,

when we bathe away preconception.
Seventy-eight percent, yet we dehydrate—

what cruel math is this? Drink a body of
water into your body of water,

be birthed from every angle, formless formed.

V. Storm

No versus. Nothing to oppose. Utopia,
how do you wear rainbows and still I can't

see you for the clouds? When rain doesn't
put out fires and wind doesn't uproot trees,

then maybe my eyes will adjust out of
necessity—nothing left to strain for.

Stacia M Fleegal is also the author of *Anatomy of a Shape-Shifter* (WordTech, 2010) and the chapbooks *The Lines Are Not My Friends* (second place, Cervená Barva Press chapbook competition, 2010) and *A Fling with the Ground* (Finishing Line Press, 2007). She was nominated for a Pushcart Prize in both 2009 and 2010. Her poems have most recently appeared in *Fourth River, The Louisville Review, Skidrow Penthouse, decomP, Pemmican, Blue Collar Review,* and *The Kerf.* She currently resides in Milwaukee, WI, and is co-founder and co-editor of both Imaginary Friend Press (www.imaginaryfriendpress.com) and the online literary journal *Blood Lotus* (www.bloodlotusjournal.com). Please visit her website at www.staciamfleegal.com.

Made in United States
Orlando, FL
14 November 2021

10416830R00060